Anonymous

The Church of the United Brethren in Christ

Represented at the World's Columbian Exposition: Chicago, Illinois, 1893

Anonymous

The Church of the United Brethren in Christ
Represented at the World's Columbian Exposition: Chicago, Illinois, 1893

ISBN/EAN: 9783743355002

Manufactured in Europe, USA, Canada, Australia, Japa

Cover: Foto ©Lupo / pixelio.de

Manufactured and distributed by brebook publishing software
(www.brebook.com)

Anonymous

The Church of the United Brethren in Christ

THE CHURCH

United Brethren in Christ

REPRESENTED AT THE

WORLD'S COLUMBIAN EXPOSITION

CHICAGO, ILLINOIS

1893

———

DAYTON, OHIO

UNITED BRETHREN PUBLISHING HOUSE

W. J. SHUEY, PUBLISHER

1893

Contents.

HISTORY AND DOCTRINE.

ORIGIN.

"UNITED BRETHREN IN CHRIST," is the title of the Church which, in the latter part of the last century, grew out of the religious awakening of William Otterbein and a number of his friends.

Philip William Otterbein, the leader of this movement, was a distinguished divine and missionary of the German Reformed Church, who was sent by the Synods of Holland, in 1752, from Dillenburg, Germany, to America. He was chosen for the mission because of his zeal and earnestness, and his deep devotion. As a young man he preached with great power and learning. It was not, however, till after his settlement at Lancaster, Pennsylvania, his first charge in America, that Otterbein, after much prayer, realized that God had poured upon him the spirit of grace and power. He now began to preach against the lifeless formality of the church, which had been thought sufficient by both ministry and people, and in the midst of which he had so long lived and worked. He therefore urged the necessity of a new birth and of experimental godliness.

While Mr. Otterbein was thus preaching, and establishing prayer-meetings, in which the laymen might have better opportunities for labor, Rev. Martin Boehm, a zealous Mennonite, having himself experienced a similar change of heart, was engaged in a different field in the same work. At a "great meeting," held about 1766,* in Isaac Long's barn, in Lancaster County, Pennsylvania, both these ministers, with many others, were present. At the close of a very earnest sermon by Mr. Boehm, Mr. Otterbein arose and embraced the preacher, crying, "We are brethren!" These words suggested, a number of years later, the name for the new denomination which finally sprang from this meeting.

From this time these brethren, with other ministers, all Germans, traveled extensively in Pennsylvania, Virginia, and Maryland, preaching to all that a vital union with Christ, in heart and life, is essential to religious growth. Otterbein himself was, in 1774, settled over a congregation at Baltimore, Maryland, which had withdrawn from the communion of the German Reformed Church. Here he remained until his death in 1813, directing and superintending the work begun in his young manhood.

It was not intended, at first, by these fellow-

---

*See *Life of Otterbein*, by Prof. A. W. Drury, D. D., pages 117-122.

workers to organize a new Church, but simply to awaken the people to the importance of conversion, or the new birth. While working with this purpose, several years passed. Later it was decided to call a conference of the ministers devoted to the work to consider the best means of uniting and establishing the believers in the new life. This gathering was held in 1789, at Baltimore, when it was decided to continue the conferences as might seem best. Finally, in 1800, the societies interested in the movement united and formed the "United Brethren in Christ," with Mr. Otterbein and Mr. Boehm as bishops.

GROWTH.

From 1800 to 1815, the Church grew slowly but steadily in the states already mentioned, its work being solely among the Germans. As many of its members emigrated to Ohio and the West, they carried forward the work, and in 1810 a new conference was formed west of the Alleghanies, known as the Miami. From this were formed, in 1818 and the years following, the Muskingum, Scioto, Indiana, and other conferences.

Among the men prominent in the movements of this and the succeeding period, besides Bishops Otterbein and Boehm, were Christian Newcomer, George Geeting, Andrew Zeller, Henry Spayth, and Henry Kumler, sr.

The zeal and devotion of these and other earnest men were abundantly rewarded.

The first General Conference met, June 6th, 1815, near Mt. Pleasant, Pennsylvania, in a small log school-house. Fourteen ministers were present, from four states. After much prayer and deliberation, the Confession of Faith was adopted, together with a book of discipline, containing rules and directions for the government of the Church.

About the same time a new period of growth began. The Church, hitherto composed exclusively of Germans, began to find earnest supporters among the English settlers west of the Alleghanies, and these conferences gradually became English. The growth was now more rapid, for the field was wider. Ministers and people were zealous in spreading their belief farther and farther. As they emigrated north and west, new churches and new conferences were formed, and the succeeding decades showed marked growth. The Church, which in 1820 had about one hundred and fourteen preachers, with thirty-six itinerants, and perhaps ten thousand members, included in 1845 five hundred and eighty-one preachers and about thirty-six thousand members.

In the earlier years John Russel, Joseph Hoffman, John McNamar, and others, and in the later years Wm. Davis, J. Griffith, W. R. Rhinehart, J. J. Glossbrenner, D. Edwards, and many others contributed to the establishment of the work of the Church and of its principles. This was the period in which the position of the Church was taken on many of the great moral questions which distinguish it; and the men of the time were worthy of the work.

The efforts of the Church during these years were largely expended in the country districts, the ministers for some reason avoiding the towns and cities. Each itinerant had many appointments, traveling from one to another, preaching at private houses, in barns, school-houses, or wherever opportunity offered. His salary was small, often but a few dollars, but he was always honored, and the people everywhere received him with kindness and hospitality.

The increasing growth of the Church led to the adoption, by the General Conference of 1841, of the Constitution, which from that time till 1889 was the basis of the legislation of the various general conferences. This same growth had led to the establishment, in 1834, of the *Religious Telescope*, and the beginning of the Publishing House of the Church. It was but a little later, in 1845, that the first steps in our educational history were taken, and the first college was opened in 1847. But progress was not yet stopped. Feeling that the Church is to carry the gospel to all the earth, the Missionary Society was organized in 1853, and the first missionaries were appointed a year later. In 1875 the women of the Church began their active, aggressive work in the Woman's Missionary Association. From the early catechetical schools had come the Sunday-schools, first organized about 1827. To supply their wants were begun the *Children's Friend* and *Missionary Visitor*, and later the various Bible lesson-helps, now so important a part of our work.

In response to the evident desire of a large part of the Church for some improvements in its government, the General Conference of 1885 appointed a Commission of twenty-seven ministers and laymen "to consider our present Confession of Faith and Constitution, and prepare such a form of belief and such amended fundamental rules for the government of this Church in the future as will, in their judgment, be best adapted to secure its growth and efficiency in the work of evangelizing the world." Certain limitations were at the same time placed upon the Commission. It was also to present its report to the Church for approval or rejection by the members. This Commission met in 1885, made a series of changes, and determined upon a plan for submitting them to the Church. For nearly three years the subject was debated, and in November, 1888, by a vote of the requisite number of the members, the forms submitted were adopted. By the announcement of the General Conference of 1889, these became the expression of faith and the law of the Church on May 13th, of that year.

During the later years, the Church has been occupied in the development of the various departments of its work. Many of the men who have been influential in these movements are still living, earnest in their endeavors, and honored by their fellow-men. The growth continues, the efforts to hold the early zeal and devotion are unbroken, and the mission of the Church—to maintain decided positions on all questions of Christian life—is daily fulfilled in the work of its people. In 1888 there were fourteen hundred and ninety itinerants, with two hundred and four thousand five hundred members, contributing over a million of dollars for church-work.

CONFESSION OF FAITH.

ADOPTED BY VOTE, 1888.—RATIFIED BY THE GENERAL CONFERENCE, 1889.

In the name of God, we declare and confess before all men the following articles of our belief:

ARTICLE I.

Of God and the Holy Trinity.

We believe in the only true God, the Father, the Son, and the Holy Ghost; that these three are one—the Father in the Son, the Son in the Father, and the Holy Ghost equal in essence or being with the Father and the Son.

ARTICLE II

Of Creation and Providence.

We believe this triune God created the heavens and the earth, and all that in them is, visible and invisible; that He sustains, protects, and governs these with gracious regard for the welfare of man, to the glory of His name.

ARTICLE III.

Of Jesus Christ.

We believe in Jesus Christ; that he is very God and man ; that he became incarnate by the power of the Holy Ghost and was born of the Virgin Mary ; that he is the Savior and Mediator of the whole human race, if they with full faith accept the grace proffered in Jesus; that this Jesus suffered and died on the cross for us, was buried, arose again on the third day, ascended into heaven, and sitteth on the right hand of God, to intercede for us; and that he will come again at the last day to judge the living and the dead.

ARTICLE IV.

Of the Holy Ghost.

We believe in the Holy Ghost; that He is equal in being with the Father and the Son ; that He convinces the world of sin, of righteousness, and of judgment; that He comforts the faithful and guides them into all truth.

ARTICLE V.

Of the Holy Scriptures.

We believe that the Holy Bible, Old and New Testaments, is the word of God; that it reveals the only true way to our salvation; that every true Christian is bound to acknowledge and receive it by the help of the Spirit of God as the only rule and guide in faith and practice.

ARTICLE VI.

Of the Church.

We believe in a holy Christian Church, composed of true believers, in which the word of God is preached by men divinely called, and the ordinances are duly administered; that this divine institution is for the maintenance of worship, for the edification of believers, and the conversion of the world to Christ.

ARTICLE VII.

Of the Sacraments.

We believe the sacraments, Baptism and the Lord's Supper, are to be in use in the Church, and should be practiced by all Christians; but the mode of baptism and the manner of observing the Lord's supper are always to be left to the judgment and understanding of each individual. Also, the baptism of children shall be left to the judgment of believing parents.

The *example* of washing of feet is to be left to the judgment of each one, to practice or not.

ARTICLE VIII.

Of Depravity.

We believe man is fallen from original righteousness, and apart from the grace of our Lord
Jesus Christ, is not only entirely destitute of
holiness, but is inclined to evil, and only evil,
and that continually: and that except a man
be born again he cannot see the kingdom of
heaven.

ARTICLE IX.

Of Justification.

We believe that penitent sinners are justified
before God, only by faith in our Lord Jesus
Christ, and not by works; yet that good works
in Christ are acceptable to God, and spring out
of a true and living faith.

ARTICLE X.

Of Regeneration and Adoption.

We believe that regeneration is the renewal
of the heart of man after the image of God,
through the word, by the act of the Holy
Ghost, by which the believer receives the spirit
of adoption and is enabled to serve God with
the will and the affections.

ARTICLE XI.

Of Sanctification.

We believe sanctification is the work of God's
grace, through the word and the Spirit, by
which those who have been born again are sep-

arated in their acts, words, and thoughts from sin, and are enabled to live unto God, and to follow holiness, without which no man shall see the Lord.

ARTICLE XII.

Of the Christian Sabbath.

We believe the Christian Sabbath is divinely appointed; that it is commemorative of our Lord's resurrection from the grave, and is an emblem of our eternal rest; that it is essential to the welfare of the civil community, and to the permanence and growth of the Christian Church, and that it should be reverently observed as a day of holy rest and of social and public worship.

ARTICLE XIII.

Of the Future State.

We believe in the resurrection of the dead; the future general judgment; and an eternal state of rewards in which the righteous dwell in endless life, and the wicked in endless punishment.

POLITY.

The Church of the United Brethren in Christ is not an off-shoot from any denomination, its founders having held in view the accomplishment of a special mission. It did not arise from differences in doctrine, for it presents no radically new doctrines of any kind. Its beliefs are those of other evangelical churches, and its theology is Arminian. It enjoins the ordinances presented by the Scriptures and followed by the Christian churches in general. Its founders united to emphasize the need of consecration of soul to God, and of personal "religious certainty," and this has been its spirit.

In its administration, it is distinguished as a body in which the power is almost equally divided between the ministry and the people. All officers hold their place by consent of the members, expressed by vote either directly or by representatives. The people choose the local church-officers, who form the majority of each official board, and the delegates to each general conference. The quarterly conference elects a lay delegate to the annual conference. The annual conference chooses its presiding elders and other officers. The general conference elects all the general officers and boards of the Church.

But one order of ministers is recognized— that of *elder*. Bishops and presiding elders are chosen from among the elders simply as superintendents.

In supplying the congregations with ministers, the "itinerant system" is the adopted method. All pastors are subject to settlement and change as determined by a committee, consisting of the bishop and the presiding elders, at each annual conference. A minister may not remain upon a charge more than three years without consent of a majority of the annual conference.

In form of worship the Church seeks directness and simplicity. It has no liturgy and does not enforce uniformity in service, each congregation deciding the method for itself.

The meetings of the Church include the regular Sabbath preaching of God's word, the weekly prayer and class-meetings, and the Sunday-school, with such others as each congregation may determine. Four times during the year the "quarterly meeting" of each charge is held by the presiding elder, at which time the general business of the charge is transacted, the communion service usually being held upon the Sabbath.

POSITION ON MORAL LIFE.

A natural result of the principles which led to the formation of the Church has been to require of its members devotion to Christ, simplicity of faith, purity of life, and uprightness of conduct. Upon all questions of morality the position of the Church has always been decided. No compromise with evil has been suggested.

The law of the Church forbids the sale or use of intoxicating liquors by its members; and the renting of property to liquor dealers, or signing a petition favoring them, is considered im-

moral. The members are always found active
in every movement for the growth of temperance. Against the use of tobacco the sentiment
is strong. Many conferences refuse to admit to
the ministry those who use it in any way.

Slavery was always thought to be a sin, and
in 1821 was entirely forbidden, the holding of
slaves being made a misdemeanor. This position has never been changed. Many members
in former days suffered severely in defense of
this principle.

The Church has always been decided in its
opposition to such secret societies as seemed to
infringe upon the rights of those outside their
organization, and to be injurious to Christian
character. Its laws have always held this in
view.

The authority of the civil government is
recognized, and the members are enjoined to
obey its laws; and while disapproving war-
fare, the Church acknowledges the obligation
of every citizen to protect and preserve the government in time of treason and invasion.

On the questions of the observance of the
Sabbath, of divorce, of the true rights of man,
the position of the Church is undoubted. Its
principles and its practice cannot fail to lead to
high Christian life.

GOVERNMENT.

CONSTITUTION.

ADOPTED BY VOTE, 1888.—RATIFIED BY THE GENERAL CONFER-
ENCE, 1889.

In the name of God, we, the members of the Church of the United Brethren in Christ, for the work of the ministry, for the edifying of the body of Christ, for the more speedy and effectual spread of the Gospel, and in order to produce and secure uniformity in faith and practice, to define the powers and business of the General Conference as recognized by this Church, and to preserve inviolate the popular will of the membership of the Church, do ordain this Constitution :

ARTICLE I.

SECTION 1. All ecclesiastical power herein granted, to enact or repeal any rule or rules of Discipline, is vested in a general conference, which shall consist of elders and laymen elected in each annual conference district throughout the Church. The number and ratio of elders and laymen, and the mode of their election, shall be determined by the General Conference.

Provided, however, that such elders shall have stood as elders in the conferences which they

21

are to represent for no less time than three years next preceding the meeting of the General Conference to which they are elected ; and that such laymen shall be not less than twenty-five years of age, and shall have been members of the Church six years, and members in the conference districts which they are to represent at least three years next preceding the meeting of the General Conference to which they are elected.

SEC. 2. The General Conference shall convene every four years, and a majority of the whole number of delegates elected shall constitute a quorum.

SEC. 3. The ministerial and lay delegates shall deliberate and vote together as one body ; but the General Conference shall have power to provide for a vote by separate orders whenever it deems it best to do so ; and in such cases, the concurrent vote of both orders shall be necessary to complete an action.

SEC. 4. The General Conference shall, at each session, elect bishops from among the elders throughout the Church who have stood six years in that capacity.

SEC. 5. The bishops shall be members *ex officio* and presiding officers of the General Conference ; but in case no bishop be present, the conference shall choose a president *pro tempore*.

SEC. 6. The General Conference shall determine the number and boundaries of the annual conferences.

SEC. 7. The General Conference shall have power to review the records of the annual conferences and see that the business of each annual conference is done strictly in accordance with the Discipline, and approve or annul, as the case may require.

SEC. 8. The General Conference shall have full control of The United Brethren Printing Establishment, The Home, Frontier and Foreign Missionary Society, The Church-Erection Society, The General Sabbath-School Board, The Board of Education, and Union Biblical Seminary. It shall also have power to establish and manage any other organization or institution within the Church which it may deem helpful in the work of evangelization.

SEC. 9. The General Conference shall have power to establish a court of appeals.

SEC. 10. The General Conference may—two-thirds of the members elected thereto concurring—propose changes in, or additions to, the Confession of Faith ; *provided*, that the concurrence of three-fourths of the annual conferences shall be necessary to their final ratification.

ARTICLE II.

The General Conference shall have power, as provided in Article I., Section 1, of this Constitution, to make rules and regulations for the

Church ; nevertheless, it shall be subject to the following limitations and restrictions :

SECTION 1. The General Conference shall enact no rule or ordinance which will change or destroy the Confession of Faith ; and shall establish no standard of doctrine contrary to the Confession of Faith.

SEC. 2. The General Conference shall enact no rule which will destroy the itinerant plan.

SEC. 3. The General Conference shall enact no rule which will deprive local preachers of their votes in the annual conferences to which they severally belong.

SEC. 4. The General Conference shall enact no rule which will abolish the right of appeal.

ARTICLE III.

SECTION 1. We declare that all secret combinations which infringe upon the rights of those outside of their organization, and whose principles and practices are injurious to the Christian character of their members, are contrary to the Word of God, and that Christians ought to have no connection with them.

The General Conference shall have power to enact such rules of Discipline with respect to such combinations as in its judgment it may deem proper.

SEC. 2. We declare that human slavery is a violation of human rights, and contrary to the

Word of God. It shall therefore in no wise be tolerated among us

ARTICLE IV.

The right, title, interest, and claim of all property, both real and personal, of whatever name or description, obtained by purchase or otherwise, by any person or persons, for the use, benefit and behoof of the Church of the United Brethren in Christ, are hereby fully recognized, and held to vest in the Church aforesaid.

ARTICLE V.

SECTION 1. Amendments to this Constitution may be proposed by any General Conference,—two-thirds of the members elected thereto concurring,—which amendments shall be submitted to a vote of the membership throughout the Church, under regulations authorized by said conference.

A majority of all the votes cast upon any submitted amendment shall be necessary to its final ratification.

SEC. 2. The foregoing amended Constitution shall be in force from and after the first Monday after the second Thursday of May, 1889, upon official proclamation thereof by the Board of Bishops ; *provided*, that the General Conference elected for 1889 shall be the lawful legislative body under the amended Constitution, with full power, until its final adjournment, to enact such rules as the amended Constitution authorizes.[1]

[1] The foregoing pages are taken, by permission, from the "Hand-book of the United Brethren in Christ," by E. L. Shuey, A.M., in which much additional information may be found.

The following books contain valuable information in reference to the Church of the United Brethren in Christ:

"Discipline of the Church of the United Brethren in Christ." 18 mo, cloth, 25 cents.

"Handbook of the United Brethren in Christ," by E. L. Shuey, A.M. 18mo, manilla, 15 cents.

"History of the Church of the United Brethren in Christ," by John Lawrence. 8vo, sheep, $2.50.

"Our Missionary Work from 1853 to 1889," by Rev. D. K. Flickinger, D.D. 12mo, cloth, 90 cents.

"Manual of the United Brethren Publishing House; Historical and Descriptive." Profusely Illustrated. 12mo, cloth, gilt top, $1.50

"Life of Rev. Philip William Otterbein," by Prof. A. W. Drury, D.D. 12mo, cloth, $1.20.

"Life of Bishop J. J. Glossbrenner, D.D.," by Prof. A. W. Drury, D.D. 12mo, cloth, $1.25.

"Life of Bishop David Edwards, D.D.," by Dr. L. Davis, D.D. 12mo, cloth, $1.00.

For any of the above books, address W. J. Shuey, Publisher, Dayton, Ohio.

HISTORICAL AND STATISTICAL OUTLINES.

THE CHURCH.

HISTORICAL.

PHILIP WILLIAM OTTERBEIN was born in Germany, 1726; came to America as a Missionary, 1752; Pastor in Baltimore, 1774, until his death, 1813; Bishop in the United Brethren Church, 1800-1813.

Religious Movement under Otterbein and Boehm, 1766-1800.

First Conference, Baltimore, Maryland, 1789.

Church Formally Organized in Frederick County, Maryland, 1800.

First General Conference, Mount Pleasant, Pennsylvania, 1815.

Confession of Faith Revised and Formally Adopted, 1815.

First Sunday School Organized, in Corydon, Indiana, 1820.

Publishing House Established, at Circleville, Ohio, 1834.

Constitution Adopted, 1841.

First College Founded, Otterbein University, 1847.

Home, Frontier, and Foreign Missionary Society Organized, 1853.

Missionary Work in Africa Begun, 1855.

Sunday-School Association Organized, 1865.

Church-Erection Society Organized, 1869.

Missionary Work in Germany Begun, 1870.

Union Biblical Seminary Founded, 1871.

Woman's Missionary Association Organized, 1875.

Missionary Work Among the Chinese on Pacific Coast Begun, 1882.

Missionary Work in China Begun, 1889.

Amended Constitution and Revised Confession of Faith Adopted, 1889.

Young People's Christian Union Organized, June 5, 1890.

Territory Occupied, United States, Canada, and Missions in Germany, Africa, and China.

STATISTICAL.

1892.

Churches—

Organized Churches.	4,234
Ministers	2,016
Members.	203,893

Sunday Schools—

Number of Schools	3,493
Scholars Enrolled	228,024
Teachers and Officers	33,895
Whole Number in Schools.	261,919
Conversions in Sunday Schools	8,042

Missions—

Home Missions.	351
Home Missionaries.	333
Foreign Missions	39
Foreign Missionaries, American	23
Native	45

Educational—

Colleges and Academies	17
Theological Seminaries	1
Professors and Instructors......................	161
Students	3,089

Finances—

Collected for Missions..	$ 69,419
Collected for Church-Erection..............	8,897
Collected for Various Benevolent Purposes	8,715
Collected for Educational Institutions ..	36,675
Total for General Purposes	123,706
Total for All Purposes...........	1,183,030

Property—

Church Houses	2,976
Parsonages	564
Value of Churches and Parsonages	$4,933,061
Educational Property	$1,199,339
Missionary and Other Property........	$217,900
Publishing House, Gross Assets...	$346,606
Total Value of Property	$6,696,906

Growth in Membership.

1813[1] 10,000	1850[1] 40,000	1880 157,835
1820[1] 9,000	1853[1] 47,000	1890 197,123
1835[1] 20,000	1861 94,453	1892 203,893
1845[1] 30,000	1870 118,055	1893 204,517

[1] Estimated.

BISHOPS.

Rev. Jonathan Weaver, D.D., Dayton, Ohio, 1865-1893.

Rev. Nicholas Castle, D.D., Elkhart, Indiana, 1877-1893.

Rev. E. B. Kephart, D.D., LL.D., Johnstown, Pennsylvania, 1881-1893.

Rev. J. W. Hott, D.D., Woodbridge, California, 1889-1893.

Rev. J. S. Mills, D.D., Ph.D., Toledo, Iowa, 1893.

CHURCH TRUSTEES.

Rev. D. R. Miller, Hon. J. A. Shauck, Rev. W. McKee, Rev. W. J. Shuey, Rev. G. M. Mathews, John Dodds, Bishop E. B. Kephart, D.D., LL.D., Bishop N. Castle, D.D., Rev. J. W. Lilly, Rev. J. P. Landis, D.D., Ph.D , Bishop J. W. Hott, D.D., Pres. T. J. Sanders, Ph.D.

HEADQUARTERS.

The Publishing House, Union Biblical Seminary, and the offices of the various Boards of the Church are all located in Dayton, Ohio, U. S. A.

SUNDAY SCHOOLS.

HISTORICAL.

1.	Church Originated..	1766-1800
2.	First Known Sunday School, near Corydon, Indiana	1820
3.	First Sunday School in Otterbein's Church, Baltimore, Maryland..	1827
4.	First Sunday-School Song Book, Words Only..	1842
5.	First Mention of "Sabbath School" in Book of Discipline............................	1849

6. First Children's Paper Published.................... 1854
7. First Organization of Sunday-School Board
    of Managers 1865
8. First Notes on International Sunday-School
    Lessons, at Commencement of System,
    January...... 1873
9. First Sunday-School Singing Book with
    Music 1873
10. First Sunday-School Library Published 1874
11. First Sunday-School Normal Class, at Gal-
    ion, Ohio 1876
12. First Sunday-School Normal Institute,
    Chautauqua Method, Arcanum, Ohio,
    October...... 1877
13. First Children's Day, July 4 1880
14. First Sunday-School Assembly, Lisbon,
    Iowa, August 1880
15. Organization of Home Reading Circle........ 1881
16. Organization of Bible Normal Union, Oc-
    tober 19........ 1886
17. Adoption of Plan of Annual Examination
    on International Sunday-School Lessons,
    April.......... ...,. 1890
18. General Movement toward Introduction of
    Home Department in Sunday School,
    September 14 1891

STATISTICAL.

Number in Sunday Schools—

1865	78,099	1885	194,758
1870	128,842	1890	245,447
1875	160,900	1892	261,919
1880	185,960		

OFFICERS.

President—Rev. C. J. Kephart, A.M., Lebanon, Pa.
Secretary—Robert Cowden, Lit. D., Dayton, Ohio.
Treasurer—Rev. W. J. Shuey, Dayton, Ohio.
Directors—Hon. M. Edmonds, Rev. J. H. Dickson, Rev. C. J. Kephart, A.M., Rev. T. D. Adams, A.M., and Miss Estelle Krohn.

HEADQUARTERS.

Room 27, Publishing House Building, Dayton, Ohio.

HOME, FRONTIER, AND FOREIGN MISSIONARY SOCIETY.

HISTORICAL AND STATISTICAL.

Society Organized, by Act of General Conference 1853

The Board is operating missions in West Africa, Germany, Canada, and the United States. Work among the Chinese is conducted in Walla Walla, Washington. Eighteen Conferences receive aid from this Board.

Foreign Missionaries Supported...... ... 33
Home Missionaries Supported.............. 338
Total Missionaries Employed.............. 371

Sherbro Mission, *West Africa*, Commenced 1855
Two Conversions, Tom Tucker and Lucy Caulker............ 1859

Church Members in 1877   41
Church Members in 1885   1,013
Church Members in 1893   4,346
Scholars in Schools.............   486
Property in African Missions............. ... $30,600
Germany Mission, Commenced   1870
Missionaries Now Employed   10
Church Members.........   777
Churches   9
Value........ .... $14 300
Paid for Support of Germany Missions,
    1870-1893. ....,.............. ...... $39,529 09
Home Missions, Commenced...............   1853
Missionaries Now Employed   338
Church Members........   35,963
Expended in Support of Home Fields,
    1853-1893 .... $2,828,558 88
Total Expended by Society, 1853-1893.. $3,119,598 76
Endowment Fund.....................….... $85,000 00
The Organ of the Society is the *Missionary Visitor*.

OFFICERS.

President—Bishop J. Weaver, D.D.
Vice-Presidents—Bishops N. Castle, D.D., E. B. Kep-
    hart, D.D., LL.D., J. W. Hott, D.D., and J. S.
    Mills, D.D., Ph.D.
Corresponding Secretary—Rev. W. M. Bell, Dayton,
    Ohio.
Treasurer—Rev. William McKee, Dayton, Ohio.
Directors—John Dodds, Esq., Rev. G. A. Funk-
    houser, D.D., Rev. R. J. White, A.M., Rev. J. F.
    Dartmess, Rev. A. P. Funkhouser, A.M., Rev.
    A. M. Snyder, and Rev. George Miller, D.D.
Executive Committee—Bishop J. Weaver, D.D., John

Dodds, Esq , Rev. George A. Funkhouser, D.D., Rev. W. M. Bell, Rev. William McKee.

HEADQUARTERS.

The offices of the Society are located in rooms 15 and 16, on the second floor of the Publishing House, Dayton, Ohio.

WOMAN'S MISSIONARY ASSOCIATION.

HISTORICAL AND STATISTICAL

Association Organized in First United Brethren Church, Dayton, Ohio, October, 1875.

Woman's Evangel Established, 1882.

Home Organization.

Branch Societies	42
Local Adult Societies	309
Membership	6,110
Young People's Societies	38
Membership	965
Children's Bands	65
Membership	1,753
Total Membership	8,828
Total in Treasury, 1892	$21,932 29
Total Amount Collected since Organization	$143,515 20
Total Valuation of Property	$38,000 00

Mission Fields.

Bompeh, West Africa —

Established	1877
American Missionaries	8
Native Itinerants	20
Schools	5
Preaching Places	173
Members	1,434
Value of Property	$13,000

School for Chinese, Portland, Oregon—

Established	1883
American Missionaries	1
Chinese Missionaries	1
Schools	1
Enrollment	46
Value of Property	$25,000

Canton, China—

Begun	1889
American Missionaries	3
Native Missionaries	4
Schools	3
Pupils	115

TRUSTEES AND OFFICERS.

HEADQUARTERS.

Room 12, United Brethren Publishing House, Dayton, Ohio, U. S. A.

CHURCH-ERECTION SOCIETY.

HISTORICAL AND STATISTICAL.

Society Organized, by Act of General Conference   1869

Loans from Three to Five Years, Without Interest.

Congregations Aided in Building Churches Since its Organization........   207

Disbursed from 1869-1885 .... $20,374 98

Disbursed from 1885-1893 ....- $49,184 99

Total Disbursed in Twenty-Four Years....... $69,559 97

OFFICERS.

Corresponding Secretary—Rev. C. I. B. Brane, A.M., Dayton, Ohio.

Treasurer—Rev. William McKee, Dayton, Ohio.

Directors—Bishops J. Weaver, D.D., N. Castle, D.D., E. B. Kephart, D.D., LL.D., J. W. Hott, D.D., and J. S. Mills, D.D., Ph. D.; John Dodds, Rev. D. W. Sprinkle, Rev. L. Bookwalter, D.D., Rev. George Miller, D.D., and Rev. B. W. Bowman.

HEADQUARTERS.

The offices of this Society are the same as those of the Home, Frontier, and Foreign Missionary Society.

THE PUBLISHING HOUSE.

HISTORICAL AND STATISTICAL.

Founded by the General Conference, at Circleville, Ohio   1834

Original Assets $1,600

Religious Telescope First Issued, December 31 1834

Establishment Removed to Dayton, Ohio... 1853

Assets at Removal................................ $15,000

Periodicals Published at Removal 2

International Sunday - School Lessons Adopted at the Commencement of the System 1873

Periodicals Published since the Founding. 18

Periodicals Published at Present................ 13

Books and Pamphlets Published since the Founding...........................Over 300

Present Number of Managers................... 1

Present Number of Trustees.................... 9

Present Number of Editors...................... 13

Present Number of Persons Employed, About 100

Total Receipts, 1834-1893 .... $3,577,977

Book Sales, 1834-1893 .... $1,289,788

Periodical Sales, 1834-1893 .... $1,424,791

Assets $360,000

Floor Space, More than One Acre.

PERIODICALS.

Religious Telescope, Established 1834

Froehliche Botschafter, Established.......... 1840

Children's Friend, Established............... 1854

Missionary Visitor, Established.............. 1865

Der Jugend Pilger, Established 1870

Our Intermediate Bible-Lesson Quarterly, Established 1873

Our Bible Teacher, Established............. 1873

Lessons for the Little Ones, Established... 1876

Our Bible-Lesson Quarterly, Established.. 1879

Woman's Evangel, Established 1882

Quarterly Review, Established   1890

Sonntagschul-Lectionen, Established.........   1890

Young People's Paper, Established....   1893

Present Aggregate Circulation of the Above   343,297

Total Number of *Copies* Issued in 1892-

    1893.........   6,774,700

EDITORS.

Editor of the *Religious Telescope*, Rev. I. L. Kephart, D D., F. S. Sc., 1889-1893.

Associate Editor of the *Religious Telescope*, Rev. M. R. Drury, D D., 1881-1893.

Editor of Sunday-School Literature, Rev. J. W. Etter, D.D., 1893.

Associate Editor of Sunday-School Literature, Rev. H. A. Thompson, D.D., LL.D., 1893.

Editors of *Quarterly Review*, Professors G. A. Funkhouser, D.D., J P. Landis, D.D., Ph. D., A. W. Drury, D.D., and S. D. Faust, A.M.

Editor of Young People's Paper, Rev. H. F. Shupe, Dayton, Ohio

Editor of German Periodicals, Rev E. Light, 1885-1889, 1893.

Editor of *Missionary Visitor*, Rev. W. M. Bell, 1893.

Editor of *Woman's Evangel*, Mrs. L. R. Keister, M.A., 1882-1893.

Associate Editor of *Woman's Evangel*, Mrs. L. K. Miller, M.A., 1888-1893

PUBLISHER.

Rev. W. J. Shuey, 1864-1893.

TRUSTEES.

Rev. George Miller, D.D., D. L. Rike, Rev. G. M. Mathews, John Dodds. *Local Committee*—D. L. Rike, John Dodds, Rev. G. M Mathews.

LOCATION.

The Publishing House is situated on the northeast corner of Main and Fourth Streets, Dayton, Ohio, U. S. A. The location is the most desirable in the city.

EDUCATIONAL WORK.

HISTORICAL.

First College Founded, Otterbein University, at Westerville, Ohio, 1847.

Board of Education Organized, 1869.

Union Biblical Seminary Founded at Dayton, Ohio, 1871.

STATISTICAL, 1891-92.

Colleges.	11
Academies	6
Theological Seminaries.	1
Total Number of Educational Institutions..	18
Professors and Instructors	161
Students	3,089
Theological Students in Union Biblical Seminary (Included in the Above)	53
Graduates Over	1,200
Students Studying for the Ministry	176
Converted During the Year	187
Buildings	33
Value of Buildings	$492,600
Endowments	$436,624
Contingent Assets	$228,480
Cabinets and Furniture	$21,955

Volumes in Libraries........................... 23,210
Value of Libraries $17,550
Beneficiary Fund............................... ... $2,130
Beneficiary Students.......... 26
Total Value of Educational Property $1,199,339
Indebtedness $326,530
Net Value $872,809
Collected for Educational Purposes in 1891-92 $38,223

INSTITUTIONS.

	Founded.	Profs. & Inst'rs.	Students.
Otterbein University, Westerville, Ohio; President, Rev. T. J. Sanders, Ph. D........	1847	14	301
Western College, Toledo, Iowa; President, Rev. A. M. Beal, A.M........	1856	25	409
Westfield College, Westfield, Illinois; President, Rev. W. H. Klinefelter, D.D	1865	8	191
Lane University, Lecompton, Kansas; President, Rev. C. M. Brooke, A.M.	1865	10	178
Philomath College, Philomath, Oregon; President, Rev. W. S. Gilbert, A.M.	1865	3	70
Lebanon Valley College, Annville, Pennsylvania; President, E. B. Bierman, Ph. D...........	1867	10	116
Avalon College, Trenton, Missouri; President, Rev. F. A. Z. Kumler, A.M.......................	1869	20	305
Union Biblical Seminary, Dayton, Ohio; Senior Professor, Rev. G. A. Funkhouser, D.D........	1871	5	53
San Joaquin Valley College, Woodbridge, California; President, Rev.			

	Found-ed.	Profs. & Inst'rs.	Stud-ents.
J. G. Huber, A. M........................	1878	6	106
North Manchester College, North Manchester, Indiana; President, Rev. D. N. Howe, A.M...................	1889	10	220
York College, York, Nebraska; President, Rev. J. George, A.M............	1890	5	205
Central College, Enterprise, Kansas; President, Rev. J. A. Miller, Ph. D.	1891	10	147
Shenandoah Institute, Dayton, Virginia; Principal, Rev. G. P. Hott, A.M	1886	7	138
Fostoria Academy, Fostoria, Ohio; Principal, J. S. Wilhelm, Ph. B	1879	7	169
West Virginia Normal and Classical Academy, Buckhannon, W. Va.; Principal, W. O. Mills, Ph. B	1882	7	165
Edwards Academy, White Pine, Tennessee; Principal, R. L. Blagg, A.B.	1883	3	100
Erie Conference Seminary, Sugar Grove, Pennsylvania; Principal, Rev. R. J. White, A. M.....	1884	9	198
Rufus Clark and Wife Training-School, Shaingay, West Africa; Principal, Rev. P. Bonebrake	1887	4	18

Union Biblical Seminary.

Founded at Dayton, Ohio, in 1871, by Order of the General Conference.

Value of Buildings and Grounds.............. $40,000
Endowment $125,000
Contingent Fund $36,000
Library $3,000
Total Value of Property............................. $204,000

Total Number of Students, 1893..................   60

Total Number of Graduates   169

Faculty—Rev. G. A. Funkhouser, D.D., Rev. J. P.
Lardis, D.D., Ph. D., Rev. A. W. Drury, D.D.,
Rev. S. D. Faust, A M.

General Manager—Rev. D. R. Miller.

THE BOARD OF EDUCATION.

President—Bishop E. B. Kephart, D.D , LL.D.,
Johnstown, Pennsylvania.

Vice-President—Rev. Henry Garst, D.D., Westerville,
Ohio.

Recording and Corresponding Secretary—Rev. L.
Bookwalter, D.D., Dayton, Ohio.

Treasurer—Rev. G. A. Funkhouser, D.D., Dayton,
Ohio.

Executive Committee—Rev. H. Garst, D.D., Rev.
George A. Funkhouser, D.D., and Rev. L. Bookwalter, D.D.

Members of the Board—Bishop E. B. Kephart, D.D.,
LL.D., Pres. T. J. Sanders, Ph. D., Rev. G. A.
Funkhouser, D.D., Rev. R. J. White, A.M., Rev.
Henry Garst, D.D., Col. R. Cowden, Lit. D , Rev.
J. W. Etter, D.D., Pres. W. M. Beardshear, D.D.,
LL.D., Pres. E. B. Bierman, Ph.D., Rev. L.
Bookwalter, D.D.

YOUNG PEOPLE'S CHRISTIAN UNION.

HISTORICAL.

First Young People's Society Organized at
First Church, Dayton, Ohio................   1871

Union Organized, June 5......   1890

Special Mission Work at Los Angeles, California.

STATISTICAL—1893.

Number of Conference Unions 27
Number of Local Unions 762
Number of Members...... 30,610

OFFICERS OF THE CENTRAL UNION.

President—Prof. J. P. Landis, D.D., Ph.D., Dayton, Ohio.

Vice-Presidents—Rev. H. D. Lehman, Middletown, Pennsylvania; Rev. L. B. Hix, Muscatine, Iowa; Rev. J. W. Hicks, Fostoria, Ohio; Rev. P. M. Herrick, La Crosse, Kansas; Rev. E. A. Starkey, Los Angeles, California.

Recording Secretary—Elmer A. Runkle, Lisbon, Iowa.

Corresponding Secretary—Rev. H. F. Shupe, Dayton, Ohio.

Treasurer—Chester B. Boda, Dayton, Ohio.

Executive Council—The President, the Corresponding Secretary, Rev. W. A. Dickson, Chambersburg, Pennsylvania; E. L. Shuey, Dayton, Ohio; Rev. W. O. Fries, Fostoria, Ohio; Mrs. L. R. Keister, Dayton, Ohio; Rev. J. A. Eby, Dayton, Ohio; Miss Estelle Krohn, Galion, Ohio; Rev. M. R. Drury, Dayton, Ohio.

Editor of Young People's Paper—Rev. H. F. Shupe, Dayton, Ohio.

UNITED BRETHREN HISTORICAL SOCIETY.

OFFICERS.

President—Bishop E. B. Kephart, D.D., LL.D.

Vice-Presidents—Rev. C. I. B. Brane, A.M., Rev. G. M. Mathews.

Secretary—Rev. A. W. Drury, D.D., Dayton, Ohio.

Treasurer—S. L. Herr, Dayton, Ohio.

Librarian—E. L. Shuey, A.M., Dayton, Ohio.

Board of Managers (with above named officers)—
Bishop J. Weaver, D.D., Rev. W. J. Shuey, Rev.
I. L. Kephart, D.D., Rev. L. Bookwalter, D.D.,
Rev. W. I. Beatty, B.D.

OBJECT.

The object of the Society is to "collect and preserve information in connection with the rise and progress of the Church of the United Brethren in Christ ; also objects of curiosity and interest, in the form of manuscripts, books, pamphlets, medals, etc."

OFFICE, MUSEUM, AND LIBRARY.

The business headquarters, the museum, and library of the Society are located in room 21, on the third floor of the Publishing House, Dayton, Ohio.

THE WORLD'S CONGRESS AUXILIARY.

REPRESENTATIVES OF THE CHURCH OF THE UNITED BRETHREN IN CHRIST IN THE WORLD'S CONGRESS AUXILIARY.

COMMITTEE OF THE WORLD'S CONGRESS AUXILIARY ON A CONGRESS OF THE UNITED BRETHREN IN CHRIST.

Chairman—Bishop E. B. Kephart, D.D., LL.D., Johnstown, Pennsylvania.
Secretary—Rev. W. M. Weekley, Orangeville, Illinois.
Rev. W. M. Beardshear, D.D., LL.D., Ames, Iowa.

ON THE GENERAL AUXILIARY COUNCIL OF THE WORLD'S PARLIAMENT OF RELIGIONS.

Bishop J. Weaver, D.D., Dayton, Ohio ; Bishop J. Dickson, D.D., Chambersburg, Pennsylvania ; Rev. D. R. Miller, Dayton, Ohio ; Rev. D. Berger, D.D., Dayton, Ohio ; Rev. W. J. Shuey, Dayton, Ohio ; Rev. S. Mills, Westfield, Illinois ; Rev. George Miller, D.D., Carlisle, Iowa ; Pres. C. M. Brooke, A.M., Lecompton, Kansas ; Rev. C. Wendle, Polo, Illinois ; Rev. I. K. Statton, D.D., Cedar Rapids, Iowa ; Rev. L. S. Cornell, A.M., Denver, Colorado ; Pres. J. George, A.M., York, Nebraska ; Pres. D. N. Howe, A. M., North Manchester, Indiana ; Rev. C. T. Stearn,

Chambersburg, Pennsylvania; Rev. J. H. Snyder, D.D., Lecompton, Kansas; Prof. G. A. Funkhouser, D.D., Dayton, Ohio; Bishop E. B. Kephart, D.D., LL.D., Johnstown, Pennsylvania; Rev. G. W. M. Rigor, North Vineland, New Jersey; Rev. E. Light, Dayton, Ohio; Rev. W. M. Weekley, Freeport, Illinois; Pres. W. M. Beardshear, D.D., LL.D., Ames, Iowa; Rev. T. D. Adams, A.M., Toledo, Iowa; Rev. W. I. Beatty, B.D., Harvey, Illinois; Bishop J. W. Hott, D.D., Woodbridge, California; Bishop N. Castle, D.D., Elkhart, Indiana; Rev. P. B. Lee, D.D., Winfield, Kansas; Rev. D. W. Spinkle, Ashland, Ohio; Col. R. Cowden, Lit. D., Dayton, Ohio.

ADVISORY COUNCIL ON A CONGRESS OF THE CHURCH OF THE UNITED BRETHREN IN CHRIST.

Rev. W. I. Beatty, A.M., B.D., Chairman, Harvey, Illinois; Rev. J. W. Howe, Dayton, Virginia; Rev. C. I. B. Brane, A.M., Washington, D. C.; Rev. G. F. Deal, York, Nebraska; Pres. J. A. Weller, D.D., Ph. D., Enterprise, Kansas; Rev. F. Thomas, North Manchester, Indiana; Pres. F. A. Z. Kumler, A.M., Trenton, Missouri; Rev. J. Hill, Sugar Grove, Pennsylvania; Rev. J. L. Luttrell, Dunkirk, Ohio; Rev. J. W. Nye, Veedersburg, Indiana; Rev. H. S. Shaeffer, Gibson City, Illinois; Rev. George Sickafoose, Portland, Oregon; Pres. W. H. Klinefelter, D.D., Westfield, Illinois; Rev. A. Rigney, Adair, Illinois; Rev. G. W. Weekley, Pennsboro, W. Va.; Rev. W. N. Breidenstein, Hawkhead, Michigan; Rev. M. L. Tibbetts, Toledo, Iowa; Rev. G. W. Deaver, Deavertown, Ohio; Rev. H. Deal, Orangeville, Illinois; Rev. W. Mittendorf, Dayton, Ohio; Rev. D. F. Wilberforce, Sierra Leone, West Africa; Rev. S. J. Graham, Ade-

line, Illinois; Rev. G. H. Backus, Welland,
Ontario; Rev. E. Lorenz, Berlin, Germany; Rev. W.
H. Uhler, Lebanon, Pennsylvania; John Dodds, Esq.,
Dayton, Ohio; Rev. J. W. Lilly, Hicksville, Ohio;
D. W. Crider, Esq, York, Pennsylvania; Pres. E. B.
Bierman, A.M., Ph D., Annville, Pennsylvania; Solomon Keister, Esq., Scottdale, Pennsylvania; Rev. J.
M. Tresenriter, Adrian, Missouri.

MISCELLANEOUS APPOINTMENTS.

On the Advisory Council on a Missionary Congress,
Rev. D. K. Flickinger, D.D.; on the Woman's Advisory Council on Religious Congresses, Mrs. L. R. Keister, M.A.; on Woman's Advisory Council on Missions,
Mrs. D. L. Rike; on the Advisory Council on Higher
Education, Rev. H. A. Thompson, D.D., LL.D.; on the
Advisory Council on Congress of Historians and Historical Students, Rev. C. J. Kephart, A.M.; on the
Advisory Council on Public Instruction, Rev. L. F.
John, A.M.; on the Advisory Council on Temperance
Congresses, Rev. H. B. Dohner; on Woman's Advisory Council on Temperance Congresses, Mrs. N. G.
Whitney; on the Advisory Council on a Religious
Press Congress, Rev. M. R. Drury, D.D.; on the Advisory Council on Astronomy, President A. M. Beal,
A.M.; on the Advisory Council on Science and Philosophy, Prof. I. A. Loos, A.M.; on the Committee on
Choral Music and Training, Prof. J. F. Kinsey; on
the Committee on Organ and Church Music, Rev. E.
S. Lorenz, A.M.; on the Advisory Council on Public
Health Congress, Rev. J. L. Hensley, M.D.; on the
Advisory Council on Medical Jurisprudence, George
Wagner, M.D.; on the Advisory Council on Moral
and Social Reform, Rev. A. C. Wilmore; on Woman's

Advisory Council on Moral and Social Reform, Mrs. Jane Harper; on the Advisory Council on Farm Culture, Hon. Matt. Edmonds; on Woman's Advisory Council on Household Economics, Mrs. A. L. Billheimer; on Educational Congress, Department of Experimental Psychology, Prof. W. O. Krohn, Ph. D.

REPRESENTATIVE IN PARLIAMENT OF RELIGIONS.

Prof. J. P. Landis, D.D., Ph. D. Subject, "How can Philosophy aid the science of Religion?"

PROGRAMS.

PROGRAM FOR PRESENTATION DAY IN THE WORLD'S PARLIAMENT OF RELIGIONS, MEMORIAL ART PALACE, SEPTEMBER 14, 1893.

1. "The Origin of the United Brethren Church," Prof. A. W. Drury, D.D.
2. "The Polity of the Church," Bishop J. S. Mills, D.D., Ph. D.
3. "The Doctrine of the Church," Rev. J. W. Etter, D.D.
4. "The Educational Work of the Church," Pres. T. J. Sanders, Ph.D.
5. "The Missionary Work of the Church," Rev. D. Berger, D.D.
6. "The Sunday-School Work of the Church," Rev. H. A. Thompson, D.D., LL.D.
7. "The Attitude of the Church toward Questions of Moral Reform," Rev. I. L. Kephart, D.D.

Bishop J. Weaver, D.D., will preside. The music will be in charge of Rev. E. S. Lorenz, A.M.

PROGRAM FOR THE CONGRESS OF THE UNITED
BRETHREN IN CHRIST.

To be held September 12-15, 1893, in the First Pres-
byterian Church, Corner of Twenty-First Street and
Indiana Avenue, Chicago. Details as to hours of
meeting and manner of organizing will be published
in the Church papers.

1. The Founder of the Church, Philip William
   Otterbein—Bishop N. Castle, D.D.
2. Denominationalism Among United Brethren—
   Pres. W. H. Klinefelter, D.D.
3. The Relation of Philosophy to Theology—Rev.
   R. L. Swain, Ph. D.
4. Is Our Present Plan of Missionary Operation
   Securing Satisfactory Results?—Revs. W. R.
   Funk and W. O. Fries, A. M.
5. City Evangelization—Revs. G. M. Mathews, A.M.,
   and R. E. Williams, A.M.
6. Relation of the Social Sciences to Theology—
   Prof. G. A. Funkhouser, D D., and Prof. H.
   Garst, D.D.
7. Legitimate Methods the Church May Employ
   in the Reformation of Society—Rev. R. Rock,
   A. M.
8. Necessity of Enlarged Benevolence in the
   Church—Rev. William McKee.
9. Progressive Revelation—Rev. L. F. John, A.M.
10. The Standard of Preaching in the Church—Prof.
    B. M. Long, A.M , and Rev. J. L. Grimm.
11. The Coast District—Its Needs and Possibilities—
    Bishop J. W. Hott, D. D.
12. Should the Itinerant System of the Church be
    Materially Modified?—Revs. L. B. Hicks and
    C. T. Stearn.

13. The Educational Work of the Church.
    a. History of the Work Done—Rev. M. R. Drury, D.D.
    b. Present Demands—Pres. W. M. Beardshear, D.D., LL.D.
    c. Co-Education—Prof. Josephine Johnson.
14. Relation of Natural Sciences to Theology—Pres. A. M. Beal, A.M.
15. How Shall We Increase the Efficiency of our Sunday Schools?—Col. R. Cowden.
16. Sacred Music in the Church.
    a. Appropriate Music—Mrs. Justina L. Stevens.
    b. Schedule Music—
        1. Solo—Miss May Kephart.
        2. Choir—Miss Jennie Fearer.
        3. Chorus—Miss Susie Rike.
        4. Congregation—Rev. B. W. Bowman.
17. The Literature of the Church—Rev. W. J. Shuey.
18. Difficulties in the Way of a Rational Interpretation of the Scriptures—Mrs. Fannie Fix.
19. Pastoral Visiting as a Factor in Successful Church Work—Revs. W. M. Bell and M. S. Bovey.

One session will be occupied in the consideration of Woman's Work in the Church. Mrs. L. K. Miller, M.A., Mrs. Benjamin Marot, and Mrs. A. W. Drury will arrange the program.

Committee on Program for Y. P. C. U. day, Revs. W. A. Dickson, J. W. Hicks, and A. P. Funkhouser.